It's Okay to Not Be Okay

Written & Illustrated By
Emily Hayes

I feel **happy** when I'm running
Or riding my bike down the street.
Or when I'm at the playground,
And there are new friends to meet.

I feel **cheerful** when I'm swimming
Or playing with my sister and all of our toys.
Or when I'm eating ice cream—
That's when I REALLY feel the most **joy**.

I feel **silly** when I'm being tickled,
Or when I'm acting in a play.
I can usually be seen smiling
Several times throughout the day.

But sometimes I don't feel happy,
Not even when I'm riding my bike.
I have a funny kind of feeling
That I really do not like.

I feel a little bit **sad**.
At the playground, I play all alone.
While the other kids are having fun,
I ask my mom to please take me home.

One day, I cried and cried for an hour.
My face filled with crocodile tears.
I told my parents I wanted to be alone,
And I thought about all of my fears.

I sat in my room by myself
And hugged my knees close to my chest.
I laid my head down on my pillow,
Closed my eyes and took a rest.

I woke up to see my mom,
Rubbing my hair and kissing my cheek.
She helped me get out of bed.
I was so **tired**, my legs were still weak.

I stood up and took a stretch,
And then I hugged my mother tight.
"I was thinking about you," Mom said.
"But I had confidence you'd be all right."

"How did you know?" I asked my mom.
"Weren't you worried that I was sad?"
"Well, of course I was, my darling," she said,
"I felt really, really bad."

"Okay, well what changed then?" I asked,
Sitting back down on top of my bed.
My mom sat down next to me.
She kissed me on my head.

"Sometimes the sky is grey
And there is no reason why.
Sometimes we feel like smiling.
Other times we need to cry."

"But crying is very healthy.
It's a natural part of life.
Sadness comes and goes.
Life is not always full of delight.

"It's okay not to be okay," my mom said.
"We're not happy all the time."
"You can feel **great** and **sad** all in one day.
Experiencing a range of emotions is just fine."

Since that day, when I get sad,
I do not worry about it much.
I let myself cry if I need to,
And I'm not in a rush.

I know now **it's okay to not be okay**,
And that sometimes, I just need to let it pass.
Even on my darkest days,
I know that my sadness won't last.

So, if you're feeling like I have,
Try to find your own comfort to help get you through.
And know that **it's okay to not be okay**.
There's nothing wrong with you.

Made in the USA
Las Vegas, NV
29 May 2023

72672588R00021